It's the shortest route to success. It offers the most direct pathway to becoming a dominant player in your field. Or let's put it like this: It's one of the quickest ways to become an "alpha company."

And what characterizes an "alpha company"? We're talking about the organization that has an edge in terms of speed, quality, and cost. It's a high energy system—a company that knows how to build the corporate metabolism...how to *generate, conserve,* and *channel* corporate energy. Bottom line, it's a company that's able to compete and win.

> *What's the main argument for managing sideways?*

How can you tell if your organization qualifies? Go look at its processes. Like how you develop products. The way you serve customers. Your approach to selling, staffing, and so on.

Do these processes have real muscle? Do they cut smoothly across the different functions and work powerfully for the customer? Do they most effectively engage the time and talents of your people? Do they come together as a dynamic, cost-effective system that creates impressive shareholder value?

Managing Sideways sets forth the ground rules for becoming a process-driven organization. Follow the coaching given here, and position your company to dominate the competition.

Managing Sideways

PRITCHETT
RUMMLER-BRACHE

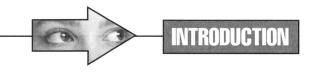

INTRODUCTION

The organization's future lies in its processes.

Tomorrow's results will be determined largely by today's approach. By the way we tackle our work.

Sure, our strategy must be solid. Our people must be capable of performing. But that won't make us competitive if our processes are clumsy.

To succeed in this demanding and chaotically changing marketplace, we have to accelerate our output. Slash costs. Bring higher quality and better value to our customers. But how do we achieve this competitive triple play of "faster-better-cheaper"? How can we build the corporate energy level and aim it toward performance breakthroughs?

The most promise will be found in process improvement.

If we scan the competitive landscape, we'll see old competitors who relentlessly keep improving. We'll be shocked at the new competition springing up from innovative outsiders who come from other fields. And we'll note that customers keep upping the ante by always expecting more.

So let's take a hard look at how we do things around here. Shall we stick with the same old habits and techniques? Or do we decide it's time to start doing things differently?

Processes are the windows into the way an organization operates. If we look there, we'll find many hidden opportunities, new passages that promise far more powerful performance. If we dig deeply into our existing methods, we'll discover the routes to dramatic breakthroughs.

The secret is to start managing sideways. The sooner the better. Because to a very large degree, our processes determine our destiny.

CONTENTS

Shift perspective 90°.

Managing in a process-centered organization calls for a new mindset. We're dealing with work from a different slant. It's no longer simply a vertical, top-down, task-specific exercise. Management now involves broad-spectrum responsibility for facilitating the flow of work from left to right. The old north to south style of management is too one-dimensional. Too localized. A process focus means our perspective must swing around such that we're mainly thinking west to east...*all the way across the company.*

Now you're managing sideways. And it's a *very* different drill.

Just as a 90° shift in wind direction announces the arrival of a new weather pattern, this quarter-circle turn on the management dial tells us we're changing the way we deal with work. Fundamentally. When we make the simple shift in focus from tasks to processes, it profoundly affects our perspective on how we do business. The different departments or functions stop operating as silos. We quit thinking of individual tasks in a singular and disconnected manner. Instead, we consider the overall collection of tasks—that is, the *process*—that's involved in producing an end result.

The old approach had us looking at our duties in a narrow-banded way, like a snapshot focused purely on our particular department or function. The rest of the organization was left out of the picture. People just paid attention to what they personally did. They didn't concentrate on process outcomes. As a result, there was a disconnect with the customer.

Not any more. We now must perceive the job like a photo taken with a wide-angle lens, one which cuts across company boundaries and reveals the full panorama of a complete work process. And the customer should always be included in this picture.

Managers—in fact, everyone—simply must pay attention to the whole. We have to concern ourselves with more than our own limited range of responsibilities. It's not enough to shine in our own small sphere. We have to look beyond, and consider ourselves personally accountable for cross-functional results. The idea is to optimize the overall process outcome, not our individual performance per se. That's especially true if we only become individual heroes at the expense of the whole. Our job is to align with others to work toward a common goal. So local agendas must be synchronized and made fully supportive of the *process.*

In this new scheme of things, people can't just do their own thing. Not even if they have a reputation for doing it exceptionally well. They have to do the *customer's* thing...the whole thing...the complete process that's in place to serve the customer. The only way we can pull this off is to think horizontally. To look laterally at how work travels across the organization. To refocus our efforts from "small and local" to "large and system-wide."

We need to make sure that all our people are mentally reoriented. That they've made this 90° shift. That they're thinking and working west to east. It's the first step toward improving the quality of process outcomes.

The organization isn't just a collection of people. It's also a collection of processes. And many of these processes have never been deliberately managed. They just sort of developed over the years. Nobody ever really took responsibility for designing them. And nobody's making sure they perform like they should.

Pick one. Check it out.

Chances are you'll find no particular person is in charge

of the process. Lots of people have their fingerprints on it,

but no single individual is accountable for overall

process results.

Is this any way to run an organization?

The job changes dramatically when your thinking shifts from managing people to managing a process.

Yeah, you're still dealing with human beings. You still carry responsibility for results. But you have to come at it very differently than before. In fact, much of what managers do in conventional organizations will actually be dysfunctional in a process-focused situation. So one of your first challenges is to *unlearn*. You'll need to abandon many of those management behaviors that made you successful in the past.

Process management requires new attitudes. New skills. You have to completely re-conceive your job. Why? Well, mainly because the people reporting to you are working at jobs which have been redrawn. Same company. Same people, maybe. But you're in charge of a different circumstance, and that naturally makes unique management demands.

You can begin by changing your point of view. Don't see yourself as the person who's supposed to make sure a department performs its tasks. Your role has broadened. You're less accountable in the vertical and local sense, but more responsible horizontally and system-wide. You're supposed to do more to shepherd work successfully across the complete end-to-end process. In fact, you'll need to concentrate as heavily on the flow of products, paper, and information *between* departments as you do on the activities within a department. You've got more to think about than just your box on the organization chart...you've got to manage the *white space* between the boxes.

Look at it like this. Your prime responsibility—your overarching assignment—is to make sure that the organization creates value for the customer. To achieve that over the long haul, you must pursue continual process improvement. That's necessary because customers get served through processes. Okay? And the best opportunities for performance gains often lie in the interfaces between departments that are working on the same process. These gaps—this *white space*— is where the baton is being passed from one function to another. It's right here that things so often get bogged down, screwed up, or lost altogether. Your job is to manage these connections. To accelerate workflow across these vacuum spots. To ensure that quality doesn't slip as a result of the handoff.

Now obviously, if you're going to be good at this, you've got to have a keen sense of the way work actually gets done. That is, how the business gets products developed. Made. Sold. Plus how they're distributed and paid for. The whole ball of wax. If you don't quite get it, how can you do all you should to help manage it? A broad grasp of the business, your customers, and the competition helps position you to engineer high-performing processes.

Final point. Good process management is about being an enabler rather than a boss. About coaching and facilitating instead of supervising and controlling. Your job is to help your people become broad-gauged and self-sufficient in problem solving. That frees you up to focus on process and to manage the *white space* on the organization chart.

How can an organization cover the ground it needs to as fast as it should?

Get rid of all that wasted motion spent on non-value-adding work. Eliminate the delays that develop in hand-off zones. Most process improvement opportunities lie at the boundary lines, both vertical and horizontal. You find them in the white space.

Bill Gates, writing in Business @ the Speed of Thought, *states, "A lousy process will consume ten times as many hours as the work itself requires. A good process will eliminate the wasted time."*

The process-centered approach gets rid of boundaries. And when the boundaries disappear, most of the busy work and delays disappear as well.

Give everybody a bigger job.

Processes work best when they're simple. You want to keep them lean, elegant, and efficient. How do you go about this streamlining? You get the complexity out of the process and move it into people's jobs.

This means the scope of people's work has to change. They need to assume responsibility for a broader range of activities. Instead of being focused on one or two single tasks, their jobs should be designed around outcomes. Toward overall end results. They must migrate from specialized labor to more general, wide-spectrum duties. This requires an expanded set of competencies. It calls for know-how in multiple disciplines. It may be that the individual needs to understand and be able to perform all the steps in a given process.

As their jobs become bigger and more complex, people need a fuller understanding of their own process and of the organization at large. They need to be able to see the big picture...how the *system* works...how all the activities in their process fit together and interconnect with other processes to ultimately serve the customer.

Everybody also needs to demonstrate sharper peripheral vision. More specifically, they have to scan the right and left horizons, taking more ownership of what happens at the boundaries before and after their individual jobs. This is the treacherous territory where disconnects are prone to occur. Where work easily comes uncoupled. Where all too often quality suffers, time slips, costs go up, and customer value gets damaged. It's here at the fringes where work enters into or emerges from the problematic *white space*.

In the new way of operating, people need to show the same level of concern for what goes on at these borders that they have for the work that goes on inside. The connection points—the handoffs—deserve as much attention as anything does. But workers naturally tend to "go bifocal," to near-sightedly concern themselves with their own special tasks. Management's job is to help them develop and maintain a broader field of view.

As jobs grow in size and complexity, work will become more interesting. More energizing. It'll get harder, too, but more meaningful. People will end up with "whole jobs," as one-dimensional work gets eliminated, automated, or folded into a bigger process.

In an organization that's *functionally* oriented, jobs have several weaknesses. Employees spend themselves narrowly on work that has been chopped into too many pieces...that involves too many people...that has too many handoffs which represent potential failure points. A *process* orientation lets them paint on a larger canvas. They're free to exercise more creative imagination. They get to engage more of their intellect. The work makes more demands of their personal judgment and problem-solving skills.

And the bottom line is that they get to grow along with their jobs.

Stop and think about it. People get paid the same whether their jobs have them doing diddly stuff or real work.

Makes no sense, but that's the business reality. In fact, it's said that 40 to 70 percent of white collar workers' efforts add no value.

How much more can you get for your payroll dollar simply by implementing good processes that eliminate non-value adding work?

In today's world, the customers run the business. Ultimately, that's who we all report to. Those people who pay the bills are the real boss, so that's who we have to please. And they're becoming more demanding, more unforgiving, with every passing day.

Since the people we serve and sell to are truly who's in charge, a customer orientation should drive all of the organization's activities. We need to start with the customers' wishes, with what they want from us, with what they consider value.

It's not our opinion that counts. As the supplier, our perspective on what represents value, quality, or worthwhile work may be quite different from the customers' thinking. But if we're smart, and if we take a process-centered approach, we'll start by determining what customers really want from us. Then we'll work backward from there.

A process is a series of related steps or tasks that together create value for the customer. The most important word here is "customer." A process perspective on a business is the customer's perspective. That's because processes are the means by which an organization produces its products and services. And the only things that customers really care about are these outputs. Our *results*. Customers are totally uninterested in our organization chart, strategic plan, personnel policies, or such. The important thing to them is the value we deliver. So if we're going to be customer-focused, we have to be process-focused.

Most processes are cross-functional. That is, they span the *white space* between the boxes on the organization chart. *Primary processes* are those that directly result in a product or service that is received by the organization's external customers. Examples could include the sales process or product development.

There also are two other types to consider. *Support processes* produce products that are invisible to the external customer. Like the recruiting and hiring process. Or the internal help desk. They go on behind the scene, but they're essential to the effective management of the business. Finally, a third category is *management processes*. This includes actions that managers should take to facilitate the smooth functioning of the business. For instance, budgeting or strategic planning.

All three types of processes, however, should be customer-centric.

A key point to keep in mind is that an organization is only as effective as its processes. In fact, over the long haul, even strong people can't compensate for a weak process. Sure, some occasional success may come from individual or team heroics. But if you pit a good performer against a bad process, the process will win almost every time.

Boiled down, what all this means is that weak processes cause weak performance. So in our efforts to serve the customer, let's first focus our people on process improvement.

Which should we be more concerned about—the quality of our products, or the quality of our business processes?

It's reported that customers are five times more likely to leave because our business processes are poor than because we have poor products.

Manage the change.

Process re-designers often follow the "field of dreams" approach: "Build an intelligent process...and they will come."

When this sort of thinking prevails, the process architects are banking on the idea that everybody will buy into the changes just because they make good economic sense. But that rarely happens. People don't automatically fall in line with a nice process, even if it's brilliantly designed.

That's understandable. Just consider what all we're asking people to do here. Comfortable and familiar ways of doing business must be ditched. Working relationships will get reshaped. Boundaries between departments need to come down. Power and authority among different functions and across levels will be redistributed. People face new performance requirements that call for new skills, different work habits, and a shift in mindset.

We're talking about serious change. And it triggers an array of very human, very predictable reactions.

You'll be dealing with confusion, fear, uncertainty, anger—feelings that generate a lot of resistance to change. In fact, it's these people and organizational issues, not the technical aspects, that present the major challenges. The behavioral side of things will be every bit as important to address as the structural aspects. And actually more difficult to deal with. Nevertheless, one of the most common mistakes is to underrate people's need to develop new mental models and behavioral competencies.

The result? Implementation efforts often drag. Maybe they fail completely, simply because not enough time or money are invested to change people's thinking, attitudes, and behavior. This sabotages the chance for the desired changes to take root. Unless people's beliefs and behaviors are altered—*significantly*—structural process changes simply won't be institutionalized.

You'll also need to align jobs with processes. Make sure that people's work is designed to support the different process steps, because organization and process improvements won't stick if they aren't built into jobs. So ask yourself how the new process stacks up against the abilities of the people who will be affected. Can they carry out the steps? Can they perform their new responsibilities?

If you decide that the process is doable, then make sure the people understand how their jobs are going to change. For example, will they have to start using a computer? Fill out different forms? Work as a member of a cross-functional team? Make higher-level decisions than they did before? Next, determine how their performance measures and goals are going to change. For example, will they now be measured on customer satisfaction? On how well they function as a team?

Everybody deserves to know what's going to change, how they'll be affected personally, and what they must do to measure up in the new scheme of things. They'll need resources and tools. Training. Constant communication and good feedback.

If people are expected to support the new process, their own new behaviors must be supported by management. We're wasting our time trying to improve workflows unless we also make changes in people's jobs, the job environment, and the way we manage them.

Process improvement implies change. And becoming a process-driven organization is big change.

Just remember that people are key to your success.

Also keep in mind that change is 30 percent logical and 70 percent emotional. The soft stuff is the hard stuff.

Put new measurement systems in place.

You're looking for a different kind of performance from your people. To make sure you get it, you must install new and different measures.

In fact, if you want to single out the one management act that can make the greatest contribution to successful and enduring process management, it would be developing and installing a process-based measurement system. Unless you do that—and do it well—you don't have a prayer of maintaining powerful processes.

Good measurement is crucial for a variety of reasons. Let's start with the fact that it signals what's important. That positions people to get their priorities straight. It focuses everybody's efforts on what counts the most. It makes it possible for them to evaluate their performance...to make improvements...to allocate their time and effort to produce maximum payoff.

Measurement provides data flow on how well we're progressing toward goals. And your job is to make sure that the right information flows, fast and accurately, to the right people. As Kenneth Blanchard puts it, "Feedback is the breakfast of champions." Measurement, by itself, is worthless. It's a poor use of time, effort, and money unless the results of our measuring are communicated to the people who can use the information.

Of course, our measurements also have to be meaningful. Timely and accurate. On the money. We don't get any mileage out of feedback if it's wrong, late, or trivial.

That brings us to the bad news: Good measures are hard to come by. But we have to nail them if we want to drive people's behavior in the right direction.

As a starting point, we must establish a set of measures that reflect the *organization's* needs. For example, the need for profitability. For effective asset utilization. For growth, innovation, and so on. These measures give us a gauge regarding how well we're doing at carrying out our strategy.

These high-level measurements then need to be broken down into related sub-measures that look more narrowly at the work being done by *individuals*. Each person needs performance measures that are more fully within his or her control. The more person-specific these are, the more powerfully they shape people's attitudes and behaviors toward producing desired results.

Finally, in addition to evaluating results at the *organization* and *individual job performer* levels, our measurement system must provide additional coverage of how well our *processes* are producing. Clearly, some of these process measures have to be based on what's important to the customer. These measures monitor the system horizontally. They're designed to assess how well we're delivering value to the customer. Ultimately, that's the key measure for the process as a whole.

Used properly, measurement is your best tool for process management. It's essential in your efforts to communicate direction, establish accountability, track performance, allocate resources, and pursue improvements. When done right, carefully chosen measures and related goals serve as the most powerful single driver of your organization's operating effectiveness as a system.

If that's not enough reason to make your measurement efforts worthwhile, keep this in mind—people want to be measured. It satisfies one of our human needs. We want to know how we're doing...how we stack up against the competition, or even against ourselves. Check it out. About the only folks you'll find who don't like being measured are poor performers.

essential that we be disciplined in tracking performance of our people and processes?

As the saying goes, "If we can't measure it, we can't control it. And if we can't control it, we can't manage it."

If we're not in a position to manage something, why would we attempt it in the first place?

Manage the environment more than the people.

Let's talk about management ROI—the return on investment you can expect from your management efforts.

What offers the best payoff? Experience proves that you'll enjoy the biggest benefits when you focus on system changes, rather than trying to improve the various people who work for you.

Nobody's arguing here against training. People definitely need coaching and development to make sure their skills measure up. The point we're making is about leverage. About playing the odds. About investing management time and energy for maximum return.

Historically, managers are inclined to over-manage individuals and under-manage the environment in which they work. They spend too much of their time "fixing" people who really aren't broken. They invest too little time fixing organizational systems that *are* broken.

The figures vary a little in different jobs, industries, and countries. But it's argued that 80 percent of performance improvement opportunities are located in the environment. Chances are only 15 to 20 percent of the opportunities will be found in the area of skills and knowledge. Finally, you can expect fewer than one percent of performance problems to result from deficiencies in people's individual capacities. The odds are overwhelmingly against the performer being the broken component of the human performance system. You seldom see a job performance "problem" that can be significantly improved by manipulating the skills and knowledge factor alone.

Again, this is not meant to discount the value of training. It's simply to bring home the critical importance of employing a systems approach to drive meaningful performance gains. After all, even talented and motivated people can improve organizational performance only as much as the business processes allow.

The dramatic performance breakthroughs occur when we concentrate on the system. When we shift our management focus from the individual's efforts to organizational performance. This comes down to taking a careful look at how work gets done and how customers get served. It's about managing the lateral movement across an organization as people perform a series of activities that accumulate to become a final output...a result. This is the horizontal system. This also is where the big problems—and great opportunities—hang out. Organizational performance usually depends most heavily on this particular environment—that is, on the effectiveness of the cross-functional processes.

This aspect of the system is what most needs and deserves management attention. As for the people, well, they need to manage themselves. They're supposed to function as self-motivated, self-sufficient performers, people who take responsibility for their own results. Instead of spending your time and energy trying to supervise and control them, invest yourself in engineering powerful processes. That's your best bet for enabling everyone to perform up to his or her true potential.

How does your company define itself? Where does it find its identity?

Maybe by the markets you serve. Or could be you base it on the goods and services you produce. But that's becoming rather old-fashioned. More and more firms are defining themselves by their processes.

Executives are awakening to the idea that their processes can be much more important than their products. Why? It's quite simple. Our processes, more than our products or services, tell us where and how we're best prepared to compete.

So take a penetrating look at your core processes. Are they powerful enough to carry you successfully into the 21st Century? Will they position you as an "alpha company"?

Encourage initiative and self-directed performance.

Let's say you've done some good architectural work on the process. You've got it designed to create value for the customer. And let's assume that people's jobs are well aligned with the process. Their performance goals position them to make meaningful process contributions.

Now what?

Now's the time to make sure you're managing sideways. West to east, mainly, rather than north to south.

Instead of supervising people, manage the *white space*. Keep your focus on the handoff zones. On results. Don't get caught up in issuing instructions, policing people's individual performance, or being too handy with helpful advice. That's the old-fashioned vertical approach. Here we're looking for horizontal management, and that means you don't want people raising issues up through the chain of command. You want them to resolve problems at *their* level. You want them to be self-directed, finding solutions on their own, operating with a high degree of personal autonomy.

This can be a big adjustment for everybody involved. Old habits keep interfering. For example, people may keep coming to you for decisions. Maybe because they honestly believe you have the best answers, or just because that gets them off the hook. Some folks may expect you to urge them on. To provide generous job structure. To be there to monitor day-to-day performance and pick up after them.

Don't do it. You've got to wean everybody from this sort of behavior. Yourself included. So long as the work group is dependent on you, the process is at risk. You're responsible for holding people accountable for the desired outcomes. Their responsibility is to deliver them. Let it end there.

If you handle your side of the situation appropriately, people will soon come to the party. For example, if you don't burden the troops with too many rules, they'll learn to improvise. If you show an appropriate tolerance for failure, they'll become willing to take reasonable risks. When you get comfortable distancing yourself from the details of how the job gets done, they'll form the habit of thinking for themselves and making their own decisions. If you'll take pains to see that they don't have to waste their time on routine and repetitive drudgery stuff, they'll have a chance to get creative and resourceful in seeking continuous improvements.

So you go first. That sets the stage for the kind of individual performance the process deserves.

Word has it that companies in the United States spend twice as much money researching and developing new products as new processes.

What's wrong with this picture?

And do you know where your organization is spending

its dollars?

Create new communication patterns.

Now that you're approaching work differently, the communication channels have to change. Information has to cut horizontally across the system, instead of following the traditional pathways up and down the organization hierarchy. A process approach must be supported by new arteries that facilitate cross-boundary communication.

Processes just don't work well when the various functions are walled off from one another. If information has to struggle up through the chain of command in one department, make it over to another area, then dribble back down that silo to the people actually doing the work, the process is far too sluggish. So the vertical communication patterns must yield to more sideways give and take. Word can get around a lot better moving laterally.

This means the slow moving routes must be bypassed. Just as an interstate freeway cuts around or over a city's clogged traffic patterns to speed travel, you have to help construct new arteries that accelerate and enrich information flow. Fast and accurate communication—across the entire process, and between processes—is crucial to performance.

You personally shouldn't be operating in the same old information loops as before. Spend your time differently. Your job is to help reduce the number of communication relay points. To focus more on communications that span the *white spaces* on the organization chart. To connect more closely with the customer and make sure the process serves the way it should.

You'll also need to upgrade the communication skills of your people, because they now carry much heavier responsibility for information exchange. While you're at it, you may need to beef up your own competency as a communicator.

If we were to single out one particular skill required of everybody in a process-centered world, it would be *communication.* The process-driven approach to work is very interpersonal. People don't perform individual tasks in a solitary, isolated fashion...they work together, in teams, performing processes. They need to be good at getting their ideas across to others. Orally and in writing. They need to know how to handle conflict. How to resolve differences. How to work collaboratively. They'll be involved in new communication patterns now, because much more of the problem-solving and decision-making will be pushed down to their level.

For your part, you also have to address the communication challenges that go with changing the way the organization operates. Remember—the toughest part of process redesign is getting people to change their behaviors and attitudes. You won't succeed without a well-conceived and sustained communication strategy.

Plan your approach to the overall change effort like you're designing a public relations campaign. You're trying to sell ideas, a new way of work. So strategize like you would before introducing a new product or when pitching some candidate for public office. Start communicating early, well ahead of any actual implementation. Help people understand the business reasons for the change. They need to know the competitive threat your organization faces. Also help them see the vision for a far more successful future. Finally, assure them of the organization's potential to improve its processes and business results.

Give thought, every step along the way, to what new communication patterns are needed to build acceptance and commitment. People will be hungry for answers. They'll be anxious and in need of assurance. You'll find them impatient for information on how they personally will be affected. Don't leave them in the dark. Either you communicate and stay in control of the story, or gossip and the rumor mill will take over. Then you're in deep trouble.

Powerful new communications won't guarantee your success at process improvement. But without new communication patterns, you're guaranteed to fail.

Communication is the oxygen that change needs to survive. Either you can provide it, or you can leave it to chance.

All too often change goes to the rumor mill to get its air supply. That provides plenty of information flow across the organization, but all the rules of gossip prevail. As a result, people end up with a warped picture of what's going on, and process improvement efforts slowly suffocate.

Here's something you can take to the bank: In any change event, some of your biggest problems will be communication problems. So make this your very top priority throughout the change initiative.

Balance the three process components: plan...perform...measure and manage.

A process requires three separate but interdependent efforts. First, there's the need for planning. Next comes performance, or execution. The third effort involves measurement and management support. The power of the overall process depends on a healthy balance between all three.

Historically, most of the effort invested in process improvement has been spent on component #2: *perform*. Organizations polish their process execution to a high sheen. They eliminate unnecessary steps. They reduce the number of handoffs. They minimize the amount of time wasted on low-value-adding work.

Eventually the process itself becomes a work of art. Problem is, this bright and shiny process that's receiving so much attention is more or less an orphan. Both the front end effort (planning) and the back end work (measurement and management support) are missing to a large degree. As a result, the process is misdirected...disconnected from the company strategy...or impotent due to a lack of follow through.

This tendency to over-focus on process execution is unfortunate. Organizations spend roughly 80 to 90 percent of their time there. But our experience suggests that the greatest opportunities for gain exist in the other two areas.

Take planning. Why invest more time and effort there? Well, this increases the odds that the process will be pointed in the right direction. It's an alignment issue. Good planning ensures that the process is linked to the organization's overall business strategy. That's essential. Because even an outstanding process can still be of very questionable value if it's off target in serving the company's higher level goals. Likewise, careful planning is necessary to link the goals of your process to other core processes in the organization. No process exists in isolation—it exists within a system of processes.

Planning also helps sort out precisely what you want a process to do. Set clear performance expectations up front, and you're in a position to measure outcomes. You need to know exactly what you're shooting for, and communicate it very clearly to all the people involved. Without that, any attempt at measurement later on is a rather worthless endeavor.

On the heels of planning and execution, the process needs measurement and management support. You analyze data. You review results. You make adjustments to improve the process' effectiveness going forward. The idea here is to dispassionately critique process outcomes, proceeding according to sound logic instead of managing by gut feel. No more going on guesswork in trying to improve the process. You rely on disciplined measurement to remove the emotion from the situation. Instead of being subjective, or playing a hunch, you can react to real problems.

Okay, so how do these duties compare with what you're accustomed to doing? Managers often struggle with what their role should be in the process-oriented scheme of things. They ask questions like, "What do *I* do? What's *my* role? How do I contribute now?" Some wonder if they'll become obsolete, since so many traditional management activities get pushed down for people to perform at lower levels.

No reason to worry. Don't disengage. There's plenty of work to go around.

You earn the paycheck now by focusing your attention and skills on planning. On measurement and management support. On synchronizing your process with the rest of the total system. It's all about managing the corporate metabolism— *generating, conserving,* and *channeling* the organization's energy supply by managing sideways.

Done right, it's full-time duty. And it positions you to contribute even more to the organization's overall success.

Managing the organization, in its truest sense, comes down to managing our processes. Day in, day out, making sure they're performing up to their potential...constantly trying to make them even better...changing them as necessary to fit our rapidly changing world.

"Faster-better-cheaper" is a moving target.

And our only chance for achieving this competitive triple play is relentless process improvement.

Turn the page and learn how to
apply these concepts in your organization